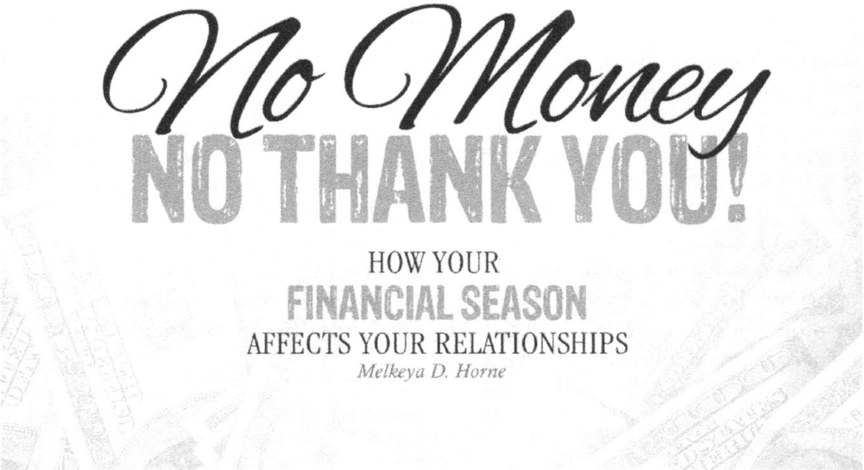

Melkeya D. Horne

No Money, No Thank You.

www.nomoneynothankyou.com

ISBN: 978-0-578-47539-4

1st Edition – June 2019

Layout & Book Formatting:
Nicholas "Redd" Scott Sr.
ServiceEqualsSales.com

Self-Published by: Melkeya D. Horne Publishing

Contact the Author of:
"No Money, No Thank You!" for Speaking, Panels, Interviews etc.
Melkeya D. Horne – nomoneynothankyou@gmail.com

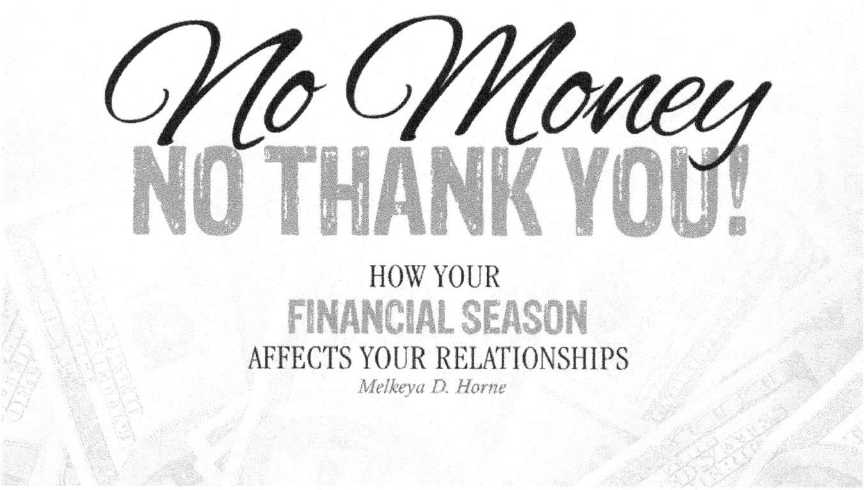
No Money
NO THANK YOU!
HOW YOUR
FINANCIAL SEASON
AFFECTS YOUR RELATIONSHIPS
Melkeya D. Horne

"They say that love is more important than money, but have you ever tried to pay your bills with a hug?" –Unknown

"Money may not buy love, but fighting about it will bankrupt your relationship." -Unknown

Table of Contents

No Money, No Thank You!

TABLE OF CONTENTS

Table of Contents

(continued on the next page)

Foreword

Foreword by Thairon Lockhart:

During the 28 years I've known my sister Melkeya, she's always been very responsible and a hero when it comes to money. She's good at managing her own personal money and has been awesome advising others on how to make better decisions dealing with their finances. Through the years, I've watched her spend within her means, balance budgets, spend frivolously and still manage to come out ahead. She's always taught me good spending habits and given sound financial advice on how to avoid going broke. Her practical tips like leaving my debit card at home, keeping cash on hand so I can physically see where my money is going, implementing 'no spending days' during the week and avoiding excessive shopping have helped me be more financially secure.

I've always thought people who understood math and numbers were not only genuinely more intelligent, but also handle their finances better. My sister has shown me I too can excel with the right tools and habits. She has instilled in me how to invest and save and be smarter with my money management and it has led me to financial freedom. You can only benefit from reading this book.

Thairon Lockhart

"...it has led me to financial freedom!"

-Thairon Lockhart

How Your Financial Season Affects Your Relationships:

Why I Write This Book:

Why I Wrote This Book:

I wrote this book so we could be candid with ourselves and reflect on how our financial seasons affect the quality of our relationships. Most of us have experienced how money can affect family; however, I'm not so sure we're honest with how our *behavior towards money* affects the relationships we choose (our friends and/or significant others). Are you dating or friends with someone who struggles financially? Sometimes it's not the "money" that impacts our relationships, rather it is how our behavior changes once we have "money."

"Money can't buy happiness, but it does provide options."

-Melkeya D. Horne

Let's Begin!

1

Financial Seasons

Financial Seasons
Winter
Spring
Summer
Fall

Financial Seasons

While reading this chapter, I would like for you to reflect and do a self-assessment of your current financial season. Life has taught me that each change in season is accompanied by changes in perception, interest and attitude. Sometimes it's evident that you're transitioning into another season and sometimes the transition is sudden and without warning.

I believe our financial seasons are synonymous with the weather's seasons: Winter, Spring, Summer and Fall. The different seasons are marked by changes in your financial position. Although, I believe financial seasons and calendar seasons are relatable, there is one thing that differs: the amount of time that each individual endures each financial season.

I will present the financial seasons the way life has introduced them to me and my circle.

Winter:

Winter is the coldest season of the year. During the winter season, your finances will either be depleted or very close to it. You will be behind on bills or barely making ends meet. No matter how hard you try, it seems as though you will always be a day late and a dollar short. There are various reasons that will make you feel like you're enduring a winter season financially.

- Loss of a job without having a sufficient savings account or at least 3 months' worth of expenses saved (emergency fund).
- Sudden illness that will prevent you from working, which in turn affects your income
- Divorce, which not only affects the adults, but the children also
- Death of the primary financial provider
- Simply having bad financial habits (i.e. excessive spending, not checking your account regularly, etc.)

My first introduction to winter was when my parents divorced during my senior year in high school and I was going away to college. I went from having money and being able to do as I wished (of course this lifestyle was provided by my parents) to barely having money at all. While in high school all I had to do was keep up my grades and I received everything I asked for. We enjoyed going to the movies and dinner every Friday night, buying CDs and movies on the Tuesday it was released and wearing whatever name brand was in style at that time. I will not reveal my age by specifying the name brands we were wearing at that time.

As I mentioned earlier, when you transition so does your perspective, interest and attitude.

During my first winter season I was excited to end one chapter of my life (high school) and start another (college). I was scared because I did not know how I was going to make it financially. Yes I had an academic scholarship, but I did not have any money for anything else. Since my parents (mom and step dad) divorced, I started to feel the financial strain. I quickly started looking for a job; whether it was work study or working off campus. I quickly discovered I was not the only one with financial issues. I developed new friendships and we were there for each other during those really hard financial times. Be mindful, some students did not have financial issues. As I matriculated throughout college, my attitude started changing. I was tired of not having money and not having the ability to do things I saw some of my peers do. School was getting harder and I was starting to think I needed a break. Some of my peers took breaks and found decent jobs. They were living life and I wanted to as well. Some of them returned and completed their degrees while others redefined their definition of success and happiness. Needless to say, I did not stop my educational journey, endured the winter season and accomplished my goal of earning my degree.

I stayed focused on school because I knew it was a temporary situation. More than that, getting a degree was a part of my idea of being successful and I wanted to be successful. Therefore, I changed my attitude from wanting to quit and kept in mind that anything worth having is worth working and fighting for.

As I got older, I was reintroduced to Winter when I was laid off from a job I had for 6 years as a Commercial Mortgage-Backed Securities Analyst. This time my perspective and attitude were different. My perspective changed because I realized I had bad financial habits. I only had a very small percentage of my earnings going to savings and I blew whatever I had left after bills. Honestly, I really can't say what I did with my money. I just know I should've had more to show for what I was earning. I noticed my temper was shorter because I couldn't do some of the things I used to do for myself and my daughter. My daughter was maybe 5 at the time. Of course, at that age it seemed like there was a birthday party every weekend and you couldn't go to a kid's party without a gift. But due to my financial winter, there were no more Chuck-E-Cheese play dates, Disney on Ice shows and unnecessary toys. After a few months my money was dwindling and I could only buy necessities and pay the bills that were absolutely necessary. I had to learn how to entertain myself and my daughter with what we already had. During this season, I could not afford to take my daughter to the movie theater so I would have to get movies from a secondary source.

Now some of us would say this is not abnormal, but I enjoy going to the movie theater. So watching movies at home took away from the theater experience. I was not at the point where I had a surround-sound system hooked up to my television. If the copy of the movie I purchased was bad, we would use our imagination and act out what we thought was happening in that scene. If we didn't watch a movie, we would play a childish game and if one of us lost the game we had to sing or dance.

Creativity will become one of your best assets during your winter season because you will have to use what you have. Winter will teach you how to endure life's dark times and reveal your substance because it did it for me. I found myself living opportunity to opportunity. It was difficult to make another career move in accounting because the market was so saturated with other professionals. I recall once literally having a bidding war on the phone in regard to hourly wages with a temp agency and another candidate to see who would take the least amount of pay. This was important because of the way temporary agencies' payroll works. For example, let's say the company where you're placed can offer $20 an hour for an employee. The temporary agency will say they can pay you $12 or $13 per hour. Therefore, the bidding war was basically about which one of us would make the temporary agency the most money by taking less. Welp for me it was another opportunity lost.

Spring:

Spring is the season when your finances are rebirthed and rejuvenated. Here are some ways you can transition from Winter into Spring:

- Tax season – Your refund (for those of us with bad financial habits)
- New job or significant salary increase

Spring introduced itself to me when I finally landed a long-term temporary position. Sounds crazy right? However, in the temp world this is very normal. As a temporary employee, I was living check to check, but I was grateful because it was income. While living check to check I decided to exercise better financial habits. Therefore, I implemented a budget very quickly. My budget was put in place by how much I bought home and the expenses that needed to get paid. While putting together my budget, I realized that certain expenses took most of my income at once and others were not as big. I started to pay the bigger expenses in portions by paying half one week before it was due and the other half the week it was due. Keep in mind, I was a temporary employee and was paid weekly. Doing this allowed me to keep money in my pocket and not have dry days. A dry day is when you have no money and are waiting on the next paycheck. I stuck to this strict budget because I'd seen how easily you can slip into a winter season and how difficult it is to get out of.

When I had money in my pocket, I also noticed I had a little more pep in my step. I did not feel as helpless as I did when I was enduring winter. I started to have goals again and my confidence was coming back, which was evident in my speech and my actions. I no longer moved timidly. One thing I noticed about having a budget was an increase in my savings. Honestly, it was not a lot at that time, however, I was happy to see a balance other than zero. During this season I also learned how to celebrate small victories. Examples of small victories were: not over drafting my account between pay periods, taking lunch and/or eating breakfast at home so I did not have to buy breakfast or lunch during the week. I also limited unnecessary driving so I did not have to keep going to the gas station. Sometimes, we get caught up just swiping our bank cards, not realizing how often we swipe them nor do we regularly check our bank accounts. By doing these things, the most important victory was having a few dollars in my pocket from the previous pay period.

While enduring spring, I had an additional financial boost with my tax refund. I could not wait to get my W-2 form to help with my financial strain. I wanted to spend that money a 100 different ways like: taking my daughter to Orlando and Disney on Ice shows, buying those expensive souvenirs they have, going shopping excessively, and eating out for breakfast, lunch and dinner. However, I did not want to fall back into a financial slump, so I continued to practice good financial habits such as sticking to my budget, meal prepping and not frivolously spending on temporary pleasures.

Summer:

Summer is the season when your finances are flowing and you have no financial care in the world. Here are some ways in which you can transition from Spring into Summer:

- Life Insurance (someone passes away and leaves you money in their will)
- Marriage – Combined Incomes
- Promotion on Job (financial increase)

After a year and two months of being a temporary employee, I was finally offered a permanent position. This meant a salary and benefits and this company had yearly bonuses. Mo money, Mo Money, Mo Money!! I was ecstatic and so relieved that my financial burden was going to be lifted. All I could think about was that I'd be able to celebrate birthdays, Christmas and any other day that required additional finances. Forget all that, I'd be able to live without penny pinching. It was a great feeling.

I started frivolously spending and going against my budget to save money. Now that I look back, I knew what I was doing was bad financial management, but it felt good to not be so restricted. I went on vacations or staycations. I started buying lavish gifts for myself. I'm a high heels girl so I would buy heels just because I saw them, but mostly just because I could. I would buy my daughter unnecessary toys and electronic games that she asked for knowing those things were not going to hold her attention long. I also started loaning family members and a few friends money although I knew that they were not going to pay me back. I said a few friends because not everyone was there to support me during my dark season. I have a whole chapter on friends where I will talk more about this. I had a hard time sticking with my budget because after some time, I had lost all financial discipline.

I had a really rude awakening when I went to swipe my card and it declined. "Wait … What?! There must be a mistake! I have money," I thought. I went and checked my account and I had a negative balance. "Oh brother, here we go; let me go back and see what in the world I spent my money on." I know I'm not the only person who bought something and took it back because the money was needed. Well after seeing that negative balance, I went and looked in my closet and took some things back I did not need. Fall introduced itself to me rather quickly and quietly.

Fall (Autumn):

Autumn, affectionately known as Fall, is the season when your finances start to slow down and you experience financial interruptions. Here are some reasons you can transition from Summer to Fall:

- Bad Financial Habits (neglect financial responsibilities to meet social expectations (standards); overspending
- Children
- Holidays (Lavish Christmas gifts, traveling to see family)
- Depleting your savings

That negative balance slapped me in the face really hard. I did not have a personal ATM who I could go to and tell them how much I needed and get it. The only safety net I had was the one I created for myself. Reluctantly, I had to go to my emergency fund to get out of the hole I created for myself. This should have been enough for me to get it together, but it wasn't. A new school year was approaching and I had to get school clothes and supplies for my daughter.

Once I got past the start of the school year, it was the holiday season so now I had a Christmas list. In order to meet all my financial demands, I started making minimum payments or sometimes even paying just what was needed to prevent disconnection. Eventually these bad financial habits – and I have no idea why I strayed from my budget – put me back into a financial bind.

After neglecting what I'd learned from my winter season, I had to get a grip on my finances so I wouldn't slip back into another winter.

Ask Yourself These Questions:

What is your current financial season?

Are you transitioning to another season? If so, which one?

Which season is your family members in and how does that affect you?

Which season are your friends in and how does that affect you?

Notes / Thoughts

2

Love Languages / Financial Love Languages

Quality Time
Acts of Service
Gift Giving

Love Languages

The author of *"The 5 Love Languages"* Dr. Gary Chapman, says there are 5 primary love languages: words of affirmation, quality time, receiving gifts, acts of service and physical touch.

Words of Affirmation - compliments or words of encouragement

Quality Time - giving the other person your undivided attention

Receiving Gifts - Gifts just because

Acts of Service - Actions speak louder than words

Physical Touch - holding hands, kissing, cuddling

These are the ways a person feels or receives love. Understanding how you, as well as your family and friends, receive and express love is a great way to maintain healthy relationships.

Just as you should be able to identify your love language, it's just as important to learn your family and friends' love languages. While dating and interacting with people, I started to notice behavioral changes when money was involved. Once I noticed behavioral changes (some were not as evident as others), I realized that people have financial love languages as well. I believe there are 3 main financial love languages: Quality Time, Acts of Service and Gift Giving. There may be other financial love languages out there but these seem to be the most communicated.

Keep in mind that some people may only speak one financial love language while others may be fluent in many. I believe it's important to learn family and friends financial love languages.

Financial Love Languages

Quality Time:

I know you're thinking, "How does quality time relate to a financial love language?" Let's think about this for a minute. You may know someone who will treat you to a nice dinner at a nice restaurant, take you on vacation with them, and take you shopping for something to wear to an event with them. This person's financial love language is quality time. This person does not mind spending money on you as long as they are in your presence or they are enjoying the event with you.

Acts of Service:

Showing love financially through acts of service takes effort and vigilance. I say this because when this language is spoken, the person expressing themselves will help relieve some of the financial pressures in your life. If this is your love language, you may be mindful of another person's financial season and help them with some expenses. You may keep gas in the car or add their cell phone bill to your plan. If an unexpected expense occurs such as a car repair, you may offer to take care of that expense. You may help pay rent or the mortgage for a few months until the financial season changes.

Gift Giving:

Those with this financial love language believe in giving gifts on any day, not just the standard holidays like: birthdays, Christmas, Mother's Day, Father's Day and/or Valentine's Day. They will give you gifts because they thought of you. If you're having a bad day, they will get you a gift to cheer you up. For major accomplishments, you will get congratulated along with a gift. For any and everything you could think of, you will receive a gift.

Through meeting new people and having new experiences, I have realized my own financial love languages are acts of service and quality time. I will be very transparent; I have difficulty with the gift giving language. Based on my experiences, if you are giving me a gift just because, and you did not start the relationship that way, then I'm thinking you did something wrong and you're trying to deter my attention from the problem. Again, this is just my perspective. There may be people out there who buy gifts just because, but I have yet to meet one. Love and financial expressions are shown in various ways based on both positive and negative examples. We normally choose which example we witnessed that yielded the best result.

One thing I believe we all have in common is we express love in the way we personally want to receive it. Now take a minute and ask yourself, "What is my financial love language?"

Ask Yourself These Questions:

What's your primary love language?

How many other languages are you fluent in?

What is your friends'/significant other's love language?

Notes / Thoughts

3

Family

Handouts
Their Personal ATM
Attitudes
Entitlement

Family

Before I was able to fully support myself, my family was a great support system. They helped me financially if they could when I came up short. For those that sacrificed meeting some of their personal needs to help me, I am truly grateful for your heart and genuine love. Not everyone could support me financially because they were going through a tough financial season themselves, but they were still a part of my support system. Some people were a soundboard to listen to me vent and give good advice, others were cheerleaders who encouraged me, and also, most importantly, there were those that kept me covered with their prayers.

I appreciate you all more than words can express. I love you!!

Change In Season:

"Congratulations we would like to offer you the position with a starting salary of $40,000. We look forward to seeing you next week Monday. For human resources purposes, can you please come in 15-20 minutes early so you can fill out the appropriate paperwork and bring in two forms of identification. Congratulations again." I recall hearing those words for the first time and how elated I was; so much so that I told my closest friends and family. I also remember hearing from family and close friends; "Congratulations. I'm so proud of you." In the next breath, they asked "So how much are you getting paid an hour? Your salary? Oh you making big money. So we are making how much a year?" I remember thinking "Wait ... What ... We? Umm I don't know how much we will be making, but I will be making $40,000." They kept at it. "So when you get your first check what are you going to buy me or where are you taking me?" Once again, I thought "Can I get my money first before you make plans for my check!!"

My first day of work I went to HR full of excitement to fill out the requested papers. I realized the W-4 form that determines how many deductions are taken (this is determined by how many people depend on this check) is the government's way of taking their money first, then giving you the remaining balance of your check. This was my first introduction to the fact that your money is not just your money.

I learned once you get your foot good in the door, then the calls start coming. "Can I borrow something and I will give it back when I can." It was no problem at all. I needed help at one time, so I obliged. The calls are not too frequent, but they are noticeable. Then I started looking at the phone like, "Are you calling to talk or are you calling to have small talk before you ask me for something?" It was family so I answered not wanting to miss anything important.

While watching one of my favorite movies "Soul Food," there was a particular scene among the sisters that I could relate to.

(Limb and Bird lovingly leave the kitchen where Teri, Max and herself were helping Momma Joe cook and the following dialogue transpired between Teri and Max:

Teri: If she spends more time getting her shop together instead of following Limb around maybe she can pay me back that money I loaned her.
Max: Teri you are not hurting that you gave Bird money for that shop.
Teri: It was a loan Max, and as far as I am concerned, I'm an ATM. Automatically Teri Money.)

I remember watching this scene and completely understanding Teri's frustration.

There is absolutely nothing wrong with helping family. I would feel a certain type of way if you did not help family in a time of need. As mentioned earlier, my family was my biggest support system before I was able to stand on my own two feet. However, there is a difference between helping family and hindering them or always expecting the person who is more financially stable to pay for things. Helping occurs when someone offers assistance of any kind because they see someone trying to better themselves and they still fall short. Hindering is when someone is not doing anything to better themselves and you support them financially and they expect you to provide because you are financially stable and able.

Expectations can create wedges between family and friendships.

I have learned that sometimes family members have a sense of entitlement to your money. You will notice the sense of entitlement when they start saying things such as: "You got it." I don't make the big dollars like you;" and my personal favorite "It ONLY costs ..." I remember a family member telling me "It only costs $150.00. My response was then you should only have it." I recall days when I did not have $150.00 to my name. Another all-time favorite is "How much did you pay for that?" In my mind, I would always think, "Why, are you buying me another one? Are you reimbursing me?"

My financial love language changed with family. At one point I expressed love by gift giving funds. You could do what you wished with the funds. After all we are adults and no one wants to be treated like a child. Then I found myself loving them with quality time. I would spend money on them as long as they were in my presence. After I changed my language, I noticed some people didn't really need the money after all. They just wanted to use my money and keep theirs. Once again, please help family. However, we don't want to hinder them from reaching their full potential. When we are in a better financial position we must learn how to discern the difference between who we are helping and who we are hindering.

Some of us, including myself, have a hard time saying no, so I learned how to set boundaries. Boundaries should be set with respect once you are self-aware.

Self-awareness - Knowing how you feel about a situation.

- I don't have to feel this way.
- Yes, I don't mind helping, but please do not take advantage of the situation. Because eventually we will all be in the same position.
- What do you want your boundary to be?

How much are you willing to lend out? Remember don't lend what you can't lose. A majority of the time, money is never paid back.

- Don't talk to me any type of way
- Identify your soft limits and hard limits

With soft limits you are willing to compromise. With hard limits, you stand firm on your boundaries.

- Most importantly, be confident in your boundaries.

Ask Yourself These Questions:

Does your financial love language change between family?

Evaluate your family. Can you identify the season they are in and their financial love language?

How many other languages are you fluent in?

Have you set boundaries?

4

Relationships

Romantic

Platonic / Friendships

Relationships

In the following chapters about romantic relationships and friendships, I would like for you to take a look into your baggage and do a self-evaluation of what finances mean to you and how they play a part in your relationships. We like to say that money is not everything, but money plays a major role in a relationship. Do you care about how much money a person makes? How long are you willing to tolerate someone's potential? Yes, it's hard to talk about finances, but I think it's time we break that stigma and talk about it.

Romantic:

When we are dating someone, we look for certain things before we become exclusive. Let me be more candid. When we are younger, we look at how they dress and how popular they are. As we mature, we look for substantial things in a partner such as what type of family they come from, if they have a relationship with GOD, health, how many kids they have, how many baby mamas or daddies, and financial stability. However, those things are based on financial love languages and financial position. One thing I have noticed is that while we are dating we never pay attention to a person's financial habits of saving or basic money management. We only see the person's spending habits. Yes, it's nice to eat at fine restaurants, take vacations, buy each other gifts and simply live your best life. However, those experiences come with a cost. In many cases we don't see what financial obligations are being neglected in order to entertain us. This small detail can cause a lot of issues later on in a relationship.

There should be a time when you openly discuss finances in a serious relationship - especially if the two of you are considering marriage. **I know it may be a hard conversation, but I honestly think it's one that needs to be had.** The conversation can also be healthy if both people are willing to be transparent, respectful of the other person's feelings and perspective and, most importantly, watch their TONE. Your tone will determine if what you're saying is being received or if that person will be on the defense. Also keep in mind that not everyone has the same experiences with money and there will be differences of opinions.

When I was younger I remember my grandmother going to pick up my grandfather's check on Fridays. Now I know this was a long time ago because now most of us have direct deposit. Even if we didn't have direct deposit, I have a very strong feeling that husbands would not have their wives picking up their checks. I could be so wrong, but I don't think that I am. Back to the subject at hand. Afterwards my grandmother, sister and myself would go and pay a few bills and then head to the grocery store. Once the day came to an end my grandparents would sit in the living room and openly discuss finances. At an early age I did not realize what I was experiencing, but I'm thankful for the example of open financial communication. I'm sure they had disagreements, but they never had them in front of me.

I think we should get back to having candid conversations about finances in serious romantic relationships. Ask what type of debt you have: student loans, credit card debt, etc. Ask if a financial plan is in place to tackle the debt. In my earlier years I only dated one person who was very candid about his finances. He had no problem saying we can't go anywhere this weekend because his funds were low due to financial obligations. I was in my early 20s so my natural responses were: "Who did you spent your money on, what happened to your money, and what type of financial obligations?" I really gave him a hard time, but now that I look back and analyze the situation, I respect the way he handled his money and he did not let my immaturity deter him.

Both parties should be involved in all money matters if it's a serious relationship, not a "situationship." Eventually, while dating someone with bad financial habits, it's likely that you will either develop bad financial habits or it can cause a strain on the relationship. Here are a few things that I think should be discussed.

- Do you believe in a budget? Do you have one in place?
- Are we creating one that's catered to our relationship?
- Is your lifestyle lining up with your actual financial situation (off brand vs. name brand)?

Believe it or not some people don't have a budget implemented and have no plans to create one. For most of us our definition of a budget is the following: "I got paid today and this bill is way past due so I have to pay this; I can wait to pay that when I get my next check." After the mandated bills are paid, we see how much money is left over and we spend until we have to implement the Rapid Budget. A Rapid Budget is when we check our bank balance and see we don't have as much money as we thought we should have. That's when we stay in the house and cook. Trust I know firsthand because I was here at one point in my life. There is no emergency fund in case a sudden expense (such as car repairs, loss of job) arises. Sometimes you don't have to ask, you can learn from people's behavior patterns if a budget is in place.

Every relationship is different and the budget should be created to tailor the needs relating to the couple's financial responsibilities. Does your partner have kids? How many kids? Children are a blessing, but they are also costly. When making plans you have to consider the kids as well. Yes, the kids have a mother and a father, but kids are a part of the package. Kids require additional expenses during certain times of the year

(Christmas, summer camps, school shopping). Will you help offset the expenses or does that responsibility fall on the biological parent? Are you talking about having kids? If so, how are you revising your budget to save for diapers, baby food, clothes and most importantly child care.

In relationships there is always one person who spends more money than another person. One person always wants to be on the scene every weekend popping bottles, wearing the newest Jordans, or having the latest iPhone that comes out, while the other person is more frugal. I'm not saying that the other person is cheap, but more careful with spending. How will you compromise with each other? Yes, it's nice to have those things, but can you afford that lifestyle? Don't get caught up trying to have the new things and you can't support yourself by taking care of life's basics: rent (mortgage), food, and utilities. More questions you should ask include:

- If you are moving in together are you splitting bills?
- Savings/Emergency Fund - Do you have one? Do you have a Financial Plan?

Separate Accounts – House and Personal

You never *really* know someone until you live with them. I used to hear that and never really understood what it meant. Baby, let me tell you that life will teach you some lessons. If you're planning to move in together, please talk about the household bills and how you both want to take care of them. Are you splitting the rent, who pays what utilities, will food costs be split, etc. I realize that "love" can serve as kryptonite to some people. Sometimes help can be mistaken for "love." You move in because y'all "love" each other and then when the financial pressure is off, they change. Move in if you want to without talking about money habits. You will acquire all types of debt. In the future, I'm checking for outstanding balances on bills, how you act when your money is low and most importantly, how you handle money. If you have too many outstanding balances, no sir you can't take care of yourself so I'm going to stay where I'm at.

While talking about bills also talk about a Savings and Emergency Fund. Ask each other, with the current income and expenses how much can we save every two weeks or monthly? This way in case an unexpected expense occurs, it will not disrupt other financial obligations that will end up putting us behind. Be mindful that sometimes things happen, and we cannot prevent them, but we can do our best to be prepared. Will you have separate accounts? It has been bought to my attention that couples have separate accounts: a house account and a personal account. The house account takes care of the household responsibilities and they have a personal account used to do what they want. If this suits your relationship cool.

A financial plan should also be talked about and established (i.e. In three months we want to have a certain amount of money saved or in a year both of our credit cards will be paid down or off). A financial plan will help you both strive to be more financially free. If you need to start with baby steps create a plan to pay all bills on time and pay any outstanding balances in three months; etc. With a financial plan, both parties have to fully commit to getting there and have discipline.

Now there are times when you are in a relationship and you feel that the other person is not living up to financial expectations based on the courting/dating phase. The honeymoon stage is always lovely. First you need to self-reflect and determine your intent on being in the relationship. Sometimes we find ourselves in relationships mainly based on material possessions and **financial status rather than the**

content of someone's character. After that's done, identify your partner's financial love language. It may not be what you assumed it to be earlier or they spoke your language to get you, but now you're in a relationship and they are speaking their true language. People can only pretend for so long. Besides "LOVE," money plays an important role in a relationship. It's one of the issues that is stressed over and it's an issue that can cause a divorce. Speaking truthfully money has power and can make you move and feel a certain way. Something I learned is that sometimes we also have unrealistic expectations. An unrealistic expectation is thinking the relationship will always be in the honeymoon stage. Another common expectation is that someone will treat you like your ex or your parents did. Basically, an unrealistic expectation is wanting someone to treat you a certain way and you can't do those things for yourself.

Hopefully, this chapter helped you realize your stance on finances in a relationship, revealed how you want finances to be handled in the relationship or served as a good conversation with your boo in regard to finances. I also hope if you're having a financial strain in your relationship, some things were mentioned that can help you see where improvements can be made and open the door for the conversation needed to resolve those strains.

Friendships

Friends are individuals with a common interest that we allow into our personal space and invest time in. As time progresses friendships evolve into something more and we no longer consider them friends, they are considered family. When friendships start, finances normally don't play a huge part. However, as time progresses, finances start play a role in things. Let me be clear. I am not saying that you will have a conversation about money before you decide if you want to be someone's friend or not. Strangely enough, the matter presents itself in many ways that we seldomly think about.

The most subtle way that finances present themselves in friendships is at dinner. You and your friends go out to eat and the waiter asks if the bill is separate or all together. What's your response? Do you quickly blurt out separate or try to be nice and say it doesn't matter? Then when the bill is placed on the table, does everyone have their phones out waiting to calculate their portion of the bill? Let me be a little more real about the meal example. Let's say when the bill comes one of your friends who had an entree', appetizer and a drink only has $20 towards the bill. What's your initial response? How do you handle that particular friend going forward? Do you stop inviting that friend to dinner, only invite them to certain restaurants or ask for separate checks when that friend is around?

Let's say that you and your circle of friends don't have this issue with the bill at dinner. That's great news. Let's say that your group of friends wants to start taking trips. How do you handle that friend that is not in a good financial season to accompany you? Do you invite that friend and take care of the expenses? Do you say next time and go without that friend?

As you transition through financial seasons your interests change because you can experience more without a tight financial strain. Take a moment to think about your intimate circle of friends as it relates to the dinner and travel examples. How do you handle each other financially? Are you all in the same financial season? If you are that is a blessing and you should be thankful.

Now ask yourself this question and be very honest with your answer: "When/if your finances change and allow new experiences how did/does that affect your friendships?" Do you exclude the person who is not financially secure? Do you invite them and cover the expenses?

Sometimes we tend to overlook genuine and authentic friendships because we no longer share the same interest. Remember friendships begin based on a common interest. It's not that we don't have those interests anymore, it's just that we sometimes don't put the same amount of energy into old friendships because they can no longer financially participate in our new interests.

If your friend is constantly struggling financially help them create a budget. A true friend will be able to handle constructive criticism. It all depends on how you present the issue to them and also your tone. Your tone of voice is very important when talking to someone about an eggshell subject.

Yes, things can happen in life and friendships come to an end. I believe that when a friendship comes to an end naturally there are no ill feelings from either individual. Normally when a separation happens, you check out of the friendship mentally before you do physically. If you are truly friends, you will help each other rise to the next level. Genuine people don't want to see friends or any one they care about struggle. Some friends are full of wisdom and knowledge from life lessons. No money in the world can replace those friendships.

There are many reasons why people develop friendships and why friendships end. Please don't let FINANCES be the primary reason a friendship ends.

I hope by reading this chapter you did a self-evaluation about some friends you have lost or relationships that are rocky. Not to say that finances played a part, but take a look at your behavior and see what part you played in the friendship ending. A sincere apology along with action behind it could possibly reunite the friendship.

Money

- Can cause conflict in relationships
- Financial issues leading cause of divorce
- Can cause stress and health problems
- Learn our money values from many sources

5

Relationship with Self

Lifestyle
Clothes
Car You Drive
Vacations
Partying
Financial Habits
Spending Habits
Saving
Paying Bills
Late Fees
Overdraft Fees
High Credit Limits

Relationship with Self

What we experienced as a child helped groom our respect for money and how we handle it as an adult. Either money was in abundance, which allowed us to experience the pleasantries of life such as themed birthday parties, lavish Christmas celebrations, name brand clothes, shoes and vacations; or on the flip side money could have been scarce, causing us to experience life's hardships such as: constant moving, overdue bills, and a few gifts on birthdays and holidays if we even celebrated at all because we were barely making ends meet. Money could have also been balanced which allowed us to experience some of life's pleasantries and hardships.

My mother gave me a real-life introduction to money and how it works by giving me the checkbook and some household bills and telling me to write out the checks. As I wrote out each check, I quickly saw how fast money came in and how fast money went out. As mentioned previously I also saw my grandparents talk openly about finances. Through those experiences, I learned very early how to handle money.

My childhood experiences were the blueprint of how I wanted my life to be as an adult. I basically wanted to live how I did as a child with a few modifications and extra perks of course. Funny how we can't wait to be adults and when we become adults, we refer to our childhood as the good times because we had no care in the world or BILLS. Although I had a good introduction to money and how it works, I was not told about the power that money possessed.

When I started to make money, I let the power of money take control and I started to move differently. Understand when you work for it you appreciate and respect money more than when it's given to you. Unfortunately, I allowed social standards to dictate how I spent my money. I was eating out for every meal every day. I was not just eating out I was eating at really nice restaurants (fine dining at its best). I must admit I still enjoy fine dining, but it's done in moderation. Instead of going to the hairdresser bi-weekly, I started going every week. Honestly, I still do this because I was not blessed with the talent of doing hair. I stayed in the mall. It was so bad I knew the days the shipment came in for my favorite stores. I had new outfits for everything and sometimes for no reason at all. If I was invited to a dinner party, I was going to the mall to purchase a new outfit, shoes and maybe even a bottle of perfume.

It felt good to be able to spend how I wanted to without any restrictions - or so I thought. I paid my bills on time, however, saving money was not on my mind initially. Eventually, I noticed that I started paying bills late because I unconsciously developed horrible spending habits.

My newly developed habits had gotten so out of hand that I needed a little financial help. I was embarrassed to ask family, so I went and found an alternative: Payday Loans. I thought this small loan would help me get back on my feet. Boy was I wrong. It's designed to be a rat race and keep having you to borrow. When you borrow from them, the interest rate is so incredibly high you end up borrowing again because you need the money. After doing this a couple of times I quickly came to my senses, revisited my budget, adjusted my spending habits and got it together. I really felt some type of way considering I went to school for accounting and finance. However, life throws us curve balls that textbooks and case studies don't prepare you for and, in the words of my college alma mater, you have to find a way or make one.

I talked a lot about myself in this chapter because I can only reflect on my experiences once I started making money consistently. I know how I felt and what lifestyle I wanted to live. I also realized that the blueprint of the life we want for ourselves is based on our upbringing and groomed by social media. The funny thing is we don't realize how fictional and dangerous social media can be. We live in a world where we are living beyond our means to impress people who don't like us, don't know us or are competing with us. We tend to become consumed with having tangible items that shows our monetary value.

Do you have boundaries for yourself? A budget?

- Savings/Emergency Fund:
  Do you have one? Financial Plan?
- Have you set boundaries for yourself?
- Can you tell yourself NO?
- Can you realize when you're spending excessively?
- Did money change you for the better or worse?

Notes / Thoughts

6

Setting boundaries to secure your financial position:

Setting boundaries to secure your financial position:

Boundaries are defined as guidelines, rules or limits that a person creates to identify reasonable, safe and permissible ways for other people to behave towards them and how they will respond when someone crosses those limits. Everyone should have boundaries regardless of what financial season you are in. Boundaries will help you maintain your current financial season and move you towards your desired season. However, it is difficult to set boundaries of any kind when you are dealing with those whom you love.

There are a few things that should be taken into consideration when setting boundaries:

Be crystal clear on your financial season

This is very important when it comes to the relationship we have with ourselves. The hardest thing to do will be setting a boundary for yourself. A lot of us are living outside of our true 'financial season trying to "keep up with the Joneses." This behavior will have us stuck in an unfavorable financial season longer than we need to be. When we are going to make an impulsive irrational decision, we excuse our behavior by saying "You Only Live Once." This is very true. We only get one life and we should live it to the fullest. However, recognizing where we truly stand financially and adjusting financial habits will allow us to live life financially free.

Hard vs. Soft Boundaries

As mentioned previously, boundaries should be set with respect once you are self-aware and truthful about your current financial season. Boundaries are key in ensuring relationships are mutually respectful, supportive and caring. Self-awareness is how you feel about a situation. No one should make you feel guilty for being financially responsible. Tell others you don't mind helping, but please do not take advantage of the situation because if they do eventually we will all be in the same financial position.

You will have soft boundaries and hard boundaries. Soft boundaries are flexible. Depending on the severity of the circumstance, you can bend on your boundary. However, be careful of those that will try to manipulate you on your soft boundary. Pay close attention to red flags such as feeling manipulated, discomfort and resentment. Say to yourself, "I don't have to feel this way. What is happening that makes me feel this way?" Once you start having those feelings, it will be a good time to re-evaluate your soft boundaries. Hard boundaries are those that you will not negotiate on. Under no circumstances should you be flexible with your hard boundary. Be careful when setting hard boundaries because they tend to be permanent. A person who has been hurt before tends to have more hard boundaries and little to no soft boundaries.

It's important to assertively and directly communicate with the other person when they've crossed a boundary. Respectfully, let the other person know what in particular is bothersome to you so you can work together to address it. With certain people, maintaining healthy boundaries doesn't require a direct and clear-cut dialogue. This is usually the case if people are similar in their communication styles, views, personalities and general approach to life. However, for those that have different personalities or cultural background, you'll need to be more direct about your boundaries.

Boundaries are all about honing in on your feelings and honoring them. If you notice yourself slipping and not sustaining your boundaries, start asking yourself, "What changed? What I am doing or [what is] the other person doing?" or "What is the situation eliciting that's making me overlook my boundaries?" Then, ask yourself "What am I going to do about the situation? What am I going to do to regain my control?" Boundaries **whether they're big or small**, are important and deserve to be respected. Boundaries aren't just a sign of a healthy relationship, they're a sign of self-respect. So give yourself permission to set boundaries and work to preserve them.

Learn to respect the power of NO

No is universal and everyone understands it no matter what language they speak. One thing that I have noticed is that no one hesitates to tell you no; but they don't want to be told NO. Learn to say NO without explanations. If you are one of the main givers it should be understood if you have to say NO sometimes. There are times when you will have to say NO in order to keep your responsibilities in line. There should be a level of comfort when saying NO. You shouldn't be so comfortable that you say no all the time and aren't willing to help. We know that it's not enough to create boundaries; we actually have to follow through with them. If a person has crossed a boundary then you should be comfortable saying no. Now when you tell someone no, please be mindful of your tone. It's not what you say, but how you say it. NO is a very small word with so much power. Use it wisely.

Notes / Thoughts

7

Check Yourself

How you treat people once your financial season has changed.

Check Yourself

How you treat people once your financial season has changed.

When your financial season changes please be mindful of how you treat others who are not in the same season you are in. I know it took a lot of hard work, discipline, and sacrifice to change your financial season for the better and you want to enjoy the fruits of your labor. Money and success have the tendency to change someone's behavior and the people around them.

Sometimes behaviors start to change unintentionally. Small condescending remarks become a part of your dialect. Honesty Moment: I was talking to my mother once and without thinking I said: "I don't like those shoes, they look cheap." She looked at me and said, "Well I like my cheap looking shoes. What you said is offensive and you should not say things like that." I apologized because I did not mean to be offensive.

Then I had an epiphany that because I did not know the brand of the shoe to determine the worth, I automatically assumed they were cheap. I had to ask myself how many times I offended someone unintentionally by making remarks of that manner. Now there are some people who will tell you what they are wearing and how much it costs without you asking. I'm not speaking of those type of people.

You may not know that you're making those types of comments, but the person being spoken to will notice. Also be mindful that you are not giving off the vibe that you're too good for certain things that you used to engage in now that your financial season has changed. You should trust the people you hang around and be open to receive criticism from them when they tell you that your behavior is changing. Realizing that you have changed can be difficult. It takes a mature person to look themselves in the mirror and admit that they are wrong and apologize.

Notes / Thoughts

Special Thanks

Special Thanks:

First, I want to thank the Lord for blessing me with this vision and placing people in my life that pushed me past my comfort zone to make this dream come true. To my prayer warrior mother *Veronica Lockhart*: I'm grateful for you praying me through this process. To my Pastor Dr. Stephanie E. Russell, thank you for your spiritual covering. To my talented, beautiful daughter *Kay-Kay*: Thank you for the pep talks and your unconditional love. To my brother and sister *Thairon* and *Trakia Lockhart*, I'm grateful for our candid conversations. *Taryn Cox*, I'm grateful for you speaking life into my dream. *Isheka Harrison*, thank you so much for all of your help and prayers. *Nicholas "Redd" Scott Sr.*, I am thankful for you and your patience. You were very persistent, pushing and pulling on my potential so that I could stop talking and start WRITING!!! I would also like to thank those that I shared my dream with who were full of excitement and support. I truly appreciate you. I would also like to thank myself for not giving up!!!

Follow Us and Share:

No Money, No Thank You!

Website:

www.NoMoneyNoThankYou.com

Instagram (IG):

@no_money_no_thankyou

Email:

nomoneynothankyou@gmail.com

I would like to personally thank you for reading my 1st Book!

Melkeya D. Horne

This book is available on Amazon.com

If you would like to purchase this book in bulk for your Team at **discounted** rates, email your request to:

Melkeya D. Horne
(nomoneynothankyou@gmail.com)

www.NoMoneyNoThankYou.com

Made in the USA
Monee, IL
04 November 2026

67381207R00056